MY JOURNEY
in a
NUTSHELL

GLORIA PATRICIA STEPHENSON

To order additional copies of this book, contact:
Xlibris
844-714-8691
www.Xlibris.com
Orders@Xlibris.com

King James Version (Authorized Version). First published
in 1611. Quoted from the KJV Classic Reference Bible,
Copyright © 1983 by The Zondervan Corporation.

ISBN: Softcover   978-1-6698-3525-7
        EBook   978-1-6698-3524-0

Print information available on the last page

Rev. date: 09/24/2022

DEDICATION

I would love to dedicate this book to the following persons:

All my children & grandchildren: You have been my greatest support and for that I am grateful. You have always been there to ensure my goals are met and I want you all to know that my womb is blessed by you. I am so proud of you all and can only encourage you to continue to soar. God bless you all.

My church family & The Unity Fasting Group of Churches: You have been a tower of strength to me throughout the years. I value you all, and the effort you place in ensuring these groups remain strong. Thank you all for believing in me, for loving me selflessly and for ensuring that the vision stays alive. I love you all.

Other Family Members and friends: The support and love you gave is so appreciated. You helped to give me the strength I desired to carry on throughout the years and I feel blessed.

MEETING JESUS AS MY SAVIOR

It was back in the 1980's when I was at my business place in Alva that I first experienced that God had a special calling on my life. I was always fearful of Him but was always delaying giving my life to Him. I remember one evening I was scheduled to go to a dance session in a village nearby where I lived then, so I prepared to attend. The truth is, my husband Aubrey did not support me going to places like these, but I thought since he was not on the island, I had no need to worry.

As I prepared my mind to attend there was a feeling of discomfort about the idea, but I kept on saying to myself, "there's no need to worry." After closing my shop late that night, I made my way up the steep hill where I was staying with my mom. There was one voice telling me about the enjoyment I would receive at the session and another voice very loudly in my head saying otherwise. For some reason the voice that was compelling me not to attend was so much louder and compelling that I lost all interest in attending and I stayed home that night.

We all retired to bed that night and while we were resting, we heard noises at the bottom of the hill. We got up to find out what was happening and saw a dark figure in the moonlight with what appeared to be a flashlight ascending the hill. My heart skipped a beat instantly and that's when I realized that the voice compelling me to stay home was not an ordinary voice. I peered through the window several times but stood motionless, and a million what ifs crowded my mind as I watched my common law husband, Aubrey, climbing the hill. He was returning from the USA, where he had gone on the farm work program.

I felt that resolve that this powerful voice I obeyed was certainly the voice of God. I knew that if I had disobeyed that voice then that would have meant maybe the end of my relationship, which has been so vital to me. I worshiped God that night for protecting me from the voice that meant me evil and vowed to serve Him. It was that specific night and many others following that I knew God had somewhat with me and believe that's where my unofficial journey with him started. I said unofficial because though I have always reverenced God and feared Him, I did not honor the vow I made then.

ACCEPTING TO WALK WITH GOD

I always feared God, and despite I could hear his voice at different points in my life, the decision to begin this journey was a bit distant. I wasn't ready to commit fully to God as I was still doing the things, "of the world." This however did not deter me from attending church services held in the community of Heartease and Alva with my friends. We enjoyed seeing the Christians clapping and singing and moving in the Holy Ghost. My friends and I would mock and laugh at times as that was basically the reason for attending at nights.

One Sunday evening however, I decided to take a walk to the church near me as this became my favourite past time. My friends stood at the window to the back of the church listening as usual, but for some strange reason there was an absolute hush of silence as we all listened to the preacher. There was something different about what I was hearing and did not even know my other friends felt the same way. After the message was done, an invitation was extended to all present who needed prayer and I did not hesitate. As I walked through the door to the altar, I could feel a sense of freedom, warmth and solace.

When the question was asked regarding who wanted to surrender to Jesus, I indicated with a show of my right hand and the rest was history. While we walked home that night, I learnt that a few of my friends had made the decision to walk with God, so the following Sunday we came prepared and were all baptized in the name of Jesus Christ. I really felt like I wasted a lot of years doing absolutely nothing of value, because the feeling I had after surrendering to God was so surreal. I started feeling like I had made such a great decision.

My husband Aubrey and I attended church together and I must let you know our lives were impacted positively and so were that of our children. We were seldom absent from church as those services served as encouragement to us. We studied the words of God together and this dedication to understanding the words of God saw him being selected to be a Bible Class teacher and a deacon in the church.

EVANGELISM

My love for God was enhanced soon after I decided to go on this route with God. I was so ignorant to many things at first, but my interest in the work of God coupled with the many men and women of God who were willing to mentor me, saw me propelling quickly.

I can recall having a great hunger and thirst for the work of God and was passionate about evangelism. Though I was just a sister in the church it did not take long before I was going on some of these missions with the ministers. We were not concerned about anything else than reaching the lost at any cost. We would journey with the late Bishop Adolphus Thomas and Pastor Mavis Whilby to Murray Mount, Sterling, Rhoden Hall, Alderton, Claremont and Gravel Hill in St. Ann to evangelize. We did not have any form of transportation to assist us, like we do today, so we traveled on foot. We would travel lightly because of the long journey and on many occasions, we would go without food. I remembered having to sleep on shop piazzas as we could not reach our destination before night fall.

I can recount on one of our evangelistic missions, we were met with very long showers of rain in the hills. We had no umbrellas like we do today, so to keep dry our only shelter was on a shop piazza or under huge rocks that were strategically placed along the roadway where we would rest and seek shelter.

I am reminded by Paul in Romans 10:14-15:

__"How then, can they call on the one they have not believed in? And how can they believe in the one of whom they have not heard? And how can they hear without someone preaching to them"? " And how can anyone preach unless they are sent? As it is written: "How beautiful are the feet of those who bring good news!"__

It is God's intent that men and women who receive Him do not stay quiet. The Lord wants us to spread His words to everyone, like Paul encouraged the Romans to do. This is how the good news of salvation will reach to the four corners of the earth so we should not allow the distance to deter us.

I can relate to the many open-air services that were used as channels to spread the words of God and to introduce Christ to the masses throughout: Alva, Heartease, Alva Line, Stephney and adjoining communities. We would identify a shop that is at a central location in a community and that is where we would have our services. By this time, I became an ordained evangelist so I would work alongside my mentors: Pastor Mavis Whilby, Evangelist Lucy Whilby and Deacon Ebenezer Wray to ensure that the members of the community knew of our intentions to visit and start spreading the good news with individuals prior to the meeting. We were not afraid to take the words to the people, but it was our joy to move out of the physical building to have services as it was our joy and constant theme to let others know about God by going to the people.

*"**Go out into the highways and along the hedges, and compel them to come in, so that my house may be filled." St. Luke 14:23**

It does not matter your class or state. The Master earnestly wants us to win souls with urgency, and that's the understanding we had. It was so fulfilling to observe men and women surrendering to God and deciding to start the pilgrimage. Today many of our ministers in the church accepted Christ on some of these missions, and I am thankful that I was on the evangelistic team.

Being on this road, I have been privileged to talk with many young people and provide support for them. I ensured I used every opportunity to speak to them about what God desires of us, and how as children of God we should walk with Him. In light of this insight, I want to use this platform to encourage all the elders in the church to be that guide for the young as they are the future, and without a future we will become extinct. Nurture the young men and women so that they can become better than us, because that's where the church will become victorious.

Proverbs 11:14 "Where no counsel is, the people fall; but in the multitude of counselors there is safety".

The evangelistic leg of my journey has been one of the most fulfilling times in my life, as I had an opportunity to see transformation happening in people's lives. My intention despite my illness is to continue seeking souls for the Kingdom of God because this is where my passion resides. God is depending on every one of us to make ourselves useful in His Kingdom. It could be praying with someone or simply encouraging a person. We must let God use us for the good of others.

St. Matthew 9: 37- 38 "Then saith he unto his disciples, the harvest truly is plenteous, but the laborers are few; Pray ye therefore the Lord of the harvest, that he will send forth laborers into his harvest".

As ministers of the gospel, we traveled to many places, and these were enjoyable times. We not only got an opportunity to know places and people but to experience God's power being manifested in people's lives. Many of the churches that exist today are as a result of the divine revelation received by the children of God back in the days and their willingness to respond to the call of God. I believe that one of the successes of the work of God in the days gone is the open mindedness of people to accept the visions and revelations of the ministers in the church. Today the church has somehow gone silent as it regards accepting and supporting individuals when they receive revelations or visions.

Solomon in Proverbs 29: 18 records, "Where there is no vision, the people perish: but he that kept the law, happy is he".

If we want to survive as children of God, we must listen to God speaking to us and execute His

divine command. This is our only true signal for direction, and we cannot sidestep this important element of our journey or else we are bound to lose our sense of direction. It is very important that we do not dilute the words of God for our own selfish gain. God is counting on us to use His words for edification and not for destruction.

On my journey some of the church services we had were held outdoors. I went to Aboukir where the Holy Ghost performed on a woman who chose to be involved in witchcraft after she was delivered through prayer. We prayed for her and stood by her while she was healed and saved from the evil spirits. God is still a healer. Women and Men of God be on your guard. Be strong, courageous and let us fight the fight of faith. Listen to His voice because He is a Counselor. Travel with Him and you will never regret a single move.

SUFFERING 'EN ROUTE ......

God did not promise that the journey would be smooth, and we wouldn't be met with really hard situations. What He promised though is that He would be with us to support us even unto the end.

When thou passeth through the waters, I will be with thee; and through the rivers, they shall not overflow thee: when thou walkest through the fire, thou shalt not be burned; neither shall the flame kindle upon thee. Isaiah 43:2

What is suffering though? You may ask?

Suffering in my own words means, 'times of hardships, trouble, extreme pain, calamity, and misfortune. Suffering happens in our physical state, and this can impact us spiritually too. In either way though the idea seems negative, however the result can be positive if we understand the state we are in and what we will learn or take away from the experience. Considering what we are going through we ask so often *"If God is all-powerful and all-good, why does He allow suffering?"* We tend to ask this question as a result of deep personal pain and not necessarily misunderstanding the fact that suffering marks the path of all humans.

We can contemplate that at the beginning of creation there was no suffering, and the Bible ends with a glimpse of newness. So, at what point did suffering come into existence?

Genesis chapter 3 records what went wrong: Adam and Eve believed Satan's lies instead of trusting God and suffering became the consequence of their sin. I really understand all that, but the human in me still wonders at times if there could not be another way.

The sufferings I have been enduring have really served many purposes and despite the physical strain on the body have helped to enhance my life spiritually. If this encourages you, even the Saviour of the world endured hardship, extreme pain and suffering too, so suffering is inescapable for us as humans. Suffering can enhance spiritual maturity, our faith in God and our walk with Him.

SPIRITUAL MATURITY & SUFFERING

There is never a circumstance I have experienced physically that has not served to strengthen me spiritually. I can let you know that being in any situation where you experience extreme pain, hardships or trouble is nothing we relish, but understanding what God promised in His words brings much assurance.

__But the God of all grace, who hath called us unto his eternal glory by Christ Jesus, after that ye have suffered a while, make you perfect, stablish, strengthen, settle you. (1 Peter 5: 10)__

Suffering by itself does not enhance spiritual maturity or growth in God, what allows that is the believers faith in God. I have extended my confidence in God despite everything that I am going through, and this first step I can say begins the process of spiritual growth. My daily reliance on God's power has helped me to focus more on what the power of God can do rather than what it can't do. My persuasion about God's grace begins with having constant dialog with God through prayer and reading His words. These are two habits we must develop if we are to stay focused on God and develop into mature individuals. It is during and after our dry seasons with much prayer and being in close contact with God that we will observe how much we transform into mature individuals. It is a fact that suffering can help to nurture us.

SUFFERING ᴇɴ ROUTE

This journey I am on as a child of God has not always been smooth sailing. I have had some great days and like everyone who is alive, there have been days when I really feel like God has forgotten me. There have been periods of joy, fulfilment, accomplishments and content, and I must also let you all know that I also experienced pockets of suffering, yes suffering.

SUFFERING AS A TEST OF FAITH

I am now going through my second series of illness, and I have tried to stay focused on God despite the pains I have at times. I would have experienced God so many times in the past and I have decided that I will continue to trust Him until I reach my destination. I am making my suffering purposeful. Using Job as my inspiration I will continue to depend on God despite how intense things may get at times. Faith is believing that something exists even when there is no visible proof.

Hebrews 11:1 "Now faith is the substance of things hoped for, the evidence of things not seen".

Reading the words of God helps to strengthen my confidence in Him because I know if I do not feed on God's promises, I will grow weak. I am a testimony of what God has done in the past so that has helped to nurture my trust in Him. I experienced healing during my first illness and that is what I use to seal the deal with God. I am going to extend my faith in Him continuously because He has been my closest friend.

<u>Romans 8: 28 And we know that all things work together for good to them that love God, to them who are the called according to his purpose.</u>

I will continue to stand firm in my confidence in God. I believe no one can endure suffering unless there is a belief that things will get better, or things will deteriorate. There must be a level of hope or trust in one's mind. If our lives are going well there is this sense of comfort and hopefulness, but as soon as we are faced with problems, pain, turbulence or discomfort we tend to get flustered or disturbed. I want to say to us all that God wants to establish our faith in Him in any situation we may find ourselves in. Is this easy to do? I will say not at first, but as soon as we make it our way of life it will get easier.

Our experiences are important in helping us to increase our trust and reliance on God. It is often said that experience teaches knowledge.

Do you remember Abraham? He had a lot of experiences that were instrumental in him becoming the father of faith.

First, he was asked to leave his country and his home. Later, he had to separate himself from Lot. The only one in his family that was with him.

Then he had to wait a long time for the birth of his son Isaac. Then when Isaac was born and had grown to be a young man, Abraham was called on to offer him as a sacrifice. Trial upon trial, one seeming to build on another. But in all of this, Abraham was strengthened in His faith and became an example to us who believe. His encounters with God provided that platform for him to understand that *"Even when we cannot understand God's plan, just trust His plan."* (Gloria Stephenson)

"………..Abraham believed God, and it was counted to him as righteousness" (Romans 4:3)

SUFFERING & HOLINESS

I have realized that we spend a lot of time paying attention to the physical battles we have to endure but seem not to understand that these are somewhat connected to the spiritual battles or warfare we are in. Let me admonish you, only those who are mature, established, strengthened and settled in Christ Jesus will be able to stand in the spiritual warfare. Christian's engagement in this spiritual battle can become really devastating if we are not aligned spiritually with God.

__Paul in Ephesians 6:12-13, states, "For we wrestle not against flesh and blood but against principalities, against powers, against the rulers of the darkness of this world against spiritual wickedness in high places. Wherefore take unto you the whole armour of God that ye may be able to withstand in the evil day, and having done all, to stand."__

How will we be able to stand against all the suffering and wiles that are placed in our lives? We must consecrate ourselves and be determined to stay clean, that's the only way our father will dwell with us and enable us to overcome our suffering.

The road I am on get dangerous at times, but I know my mind, has to be stayed on God. I acknowledge that the only cleansing agent I can use to remain sanctified are the words of God and prayer. The Lord promises to make us fit for His work, so we must meet His requirement through sanctification.

I have been suffering with pain, short of breath and more, but I am aware that in order to be victorious, my life must be holy even as Christ is holy. I must be grateful despite my situation because I have a hope in the victory of my journey that lies ahead. I know this is a part of the devil's tactic to distract me and to let me feel that God is not a healer, but I will continue to clean my vessel and endure to the end. This process of cleaning and remaining clean is not easy, but like the gold smith I am determined to use my experience to add value to my life.

Gold is valuable, and no wonder the process of accomplishing this mineral is so intense. Intense heat is placed under the smelting pot and soon after much heat, the impurities in the gold begin to rise to the top. The refiner is then able to skim the impurities off the top of the molten metal.

The more this process is repeated, the purer the gold becomes. This step in the process can be associated to the fiery trials Christians face. Though obnoxious, this step is crucial in the Christians life. Even in our furnace the skimming of the dross is necessary to build our spiritual character. Each time the heat is added the dross is removed we become so clean and valuable to ourselves and God.

In order to overcome our suffering and trials we must remember that the Refiner is waiting to skim our impurities so we can be overcomers.

I encourage us as God's children to: "Trust God's plan, even when you don't understand His plan." He wants us to be vessels of honour so we must sanctify ourselves even in the midst of our adversities so that His will may be done in our lives

"If a man therefore purge himself from these, he shall be a vessel unto honour, sanctified, and meet for the master's use, and prepared unto every good work." 2nd Timothy 2: 21

PRARYER, STRENGTH FOR THE MISSION

Prayer is the lifeline of the Christians walk with God. Without prayer you are hopeless, fruitless and lifeless. Prayer can do anything God can do.

Prayer Changes circumstances

<u>"And when they prayed, the place was shaken where they were assembled. Again, during a prayer meeting at the house of Mary, the mother of John's house, Peter was set free" (Acts 4:31 -33)</u>

Prevailing prayer by a group of believers can change circumstances around them and in them. When the disciples prayed for boldness to declare the name of Jesus to their generation, the place was literally shaken.

On another occasion, angels of God entered the prison, opened the doors and set the apostles free with instructions. ***<u>"Go stand and speak in the temple to the people all the words of this life." (Acts 5: 20).</u>*** Again, during a prayer meeting of the church in John, at Marks mothers house, an angel set Peter free from prison. Chains fell from his hands, prison doors swung open wide, and the apostle walked to the home where the prayers were being offered. We are no closer to God than the fervency of our prayer life. The privilege of being a Christian involves the responsibility to pray in faith with perseverance and expectancy. The effectiveness of prayer changes people changes the mind of God and changes circumstances.

Prayer delivered Shadrach, Meshach and Abednego from the fiery furnace. Prayer closed the mouths of the lions so they could do Daniel no harm. This consistent talk with God is urgently needed by all of us as Christians if there is the desire to complete the pilgrimage. It is what God expects of us, it is that connection He desires us to maintain if we want to reach our destination in God.

As I travel on this great mission, I have been using this same tool….' prayer." I must talk to God because He has been my closest friend.

Charles W. Fry, (1881) was inspired when he wrote the song, *"In sorrow He's my comfort, in trouble He's my stay: He tells me all my cares on Him to roll, He's the lily of the valley and the bright and morning star, He's the fairest of ten thousand to my soul."*

THE INHERITANCE AWAITS US AT THE END

After describing the inheritance as being incorruptible, undefiled not fading away and reserved in heaven for the Christians, the Apostle Peter describes Christians as those; _**"who are kept by the power of God through faith unto salvation ready to be revealed in the last time." (1Peter 1:5).**_ This promise of us receiving this inheritance is made possible because of Jesus death but is assured as a result of His resurrection.

The inheritance I am referring to is heavenly and is our hope of salvation. Unlike an earthly inheritance that is passed on through generations and sometimes causes problems this heritance is therefore not prone to decaying, fading or perishing but is reserved by Christ in heaven for us.

**To an inheritance incorruptible, and undefiled, and that fadeth not away, reserved in heaven for you (1 Peter 1:3-4).**

Not only is our inheritance guarded by God, but we are also kept by His power. God keeps the inheritance for the believer, and He keeps the believer for the inheritance. God has given every believer a proof that he will be kept unto that day when he will receive his inheritance. That proof is the Holy Spirit. God calls the proof the, "earnest of our inheritance, and is eternal in the heavens."

Like Abraham I am looking forward to seeing this city which hath foundations, whose builder and maker is God.

Hebrews 11:10 For he looked for a city which hath foundations, whose builder and maker is God.

First Peter 1:5 shows us the method God uses to keep us for our heritances. "**_Who are kept by the power of God through faith unto salvation ready to be revealed in the last time"._** We are kept by the power of God through faith. The moment we believe God, our faith is accepted by Him and with the requirements He sets for us is followed, that makes our inheritance sure. God first gives us faith my brothers and sisters. Then He keeps us by the faith He has given us.

Ephesians 2:8 For by grace are ye saved through faith; and that not of yourselves: it is the gift of God": This promise of obtaining the inheritance is not fake, but it is able to withstand any trial, sickness, or depression we face on earth.

2 Corinthians 4: 16-18 states:

"For which cause we faint not; but though our outward man perish, yet the inward man is renewed day by day. For our light affliction, which is but for a moment, worketh for us a far more exceeding and eternal weight of glory; While we look not at the things which are seen, but at the things which are not seen: for the things which are seen are temporal; but the things which are not seen are eternal".

INHERITANCE THROUGH SALVATION

The inheritance promised by God can be received by everyone who carries out the commission He gives. It entails hearing and believing the truth, accepting Christ through baptism and receiving the gift of the Holy Ghost then be determined to walk in the newness of life. These initial steps are crucial for any human being who wants to accept the Lord as Saviour or becoming a Christian. This act of receiving Christ as Father allows us to be His heirs and joint heirs.

Paul explains it well, ***"Now if we are children, then we are heirs—heirs of God and co-heirs with Christ, if indeed we share in his sufferings in order that we may also share in his glory." (Romans 8:17)***

All that God has for us is assured the moment we by faith receive Him as our Lord and Saviour. This assurance is important to all Christians so we can understand that the relationship we share with God is eternal.

TESTIMONIES OF DELIVERANCE ON MY JOURNEY

Testimony #1

As a child of God on my journey, I have many testimonies of the power of God in my Ministry.

During these years on my journey, I was so impressed with this little girl growing up. She took me as her second mother and from then we have a very good relationship.

As I reminisce on her growing up, I knew she would become a teacher and it thrills my heart to see her being successful. This young woman attended Alva Primary in St. Ann, Jamaica as a child. She was successful in her exams and was placed at Dint Hill High School, where she later matriculated to the Mico Teachers' College.

After leaving Mico Teachers' College, St. Ann Jamaica, she worked at the Crampton Primary school and then Ewarton Primary where she was later promoted as the principal of the institution. She was a young woman with a passion for education and a passion for Christ, however not many persons were happy for the strides she was making. A plot was set for her by the agents of the devil, but the spiritual foundation she was grown on allowed her to stand brave even in the face of adversity. As she continued to be faced with this situation, she decided to call on the prayer warriors, as she knew the power of prayer as was introduced to her by her mother, my aunt….or Aunt Lucy as the family would refer to her.

She invited both her biological mother, Aunt Lucy and myself to her school and we had a prayer meeting in her office. What a mighty God we serve? As soon as we started to pray the agents of the devil became confused and we started to recognize that strongholds started losing its power. Our major duty was to pray on her behalf that day, but we were so beside ourselves when people started to run to us with their children for prayer and God simply showed up in that facility. The haters were there but the Power of Prayer was stronger than what they had. We felt the strongholds of the enemy started crumbling. Not many days following, God destroyed the plot that the enemy placed on her. Today she is alive and remains a testimony of what the Holy Spirit and the anointing of God can do. Mrs. Marjorie Bailey, my daughter, fought many battles but because she is covered under the blood of Jesus, she continues to be safe, she continues to be a powerful woman of God, and I am a witness of how God delivered her.

Testimony # 2

It is indeed a fact that when we pray, shackles will have to be broken then we can be delivered. I remember as a mother growing my children it was not an easy feat. My husband and I had nine children and I can tell you all that it was not easy on us, but we did it. As a family we were not always comfortable, but as parents we tried to teach all our children the importance of loving the Lord, relying on Him wherever they go, or in whatever situation they are faced with. It is always the norm for all my children to come to me to be prayed for when they are leaving for school, for an interview or any occasion they must pursue. This was the norm I created in my family, and I am happy I did that because I have seen God working through this strategy I implemented. I did not even realize how powerful this would have impacted my family, but I can testify that through prayer my children testify that they too experience the power of God in their lives.

As my children grow and mature in God, I also observe them taking their children to me to be prayed for too. I am happy they recognized the many miracles God worked through those prayers and I am also happy they experienced God for themselves too. My brothers and sisters this is one of the greatest legacy you can give to your family, introducing them to God and the importance of prayer.

I can testify of the many times God showed up in my life by making provision for my children. After my husband passed things were not easy for me to provide for my family, but I trusted God so much that He showed up in my life. I believed I was working for God so in return He made provisions for my family and me. In addition to using my hands in a creative way to earn a living, God helped me to pay the school fees and other expenses related to school amd everyday living were always taken care of one way or another.

I am happy all my children were introduced to God from a tender age. I ensured that they were taken to Sunday school and encouraged them to participate actively in the church. They saw the path I chose and witnessed firsthand the wonderful work God called me to perform for His kingdom and many of them followed.

This is the best gift any parent can give to a child…. Christ.

2ⁿᵈ Timothy 3:14-16

"But continue thou in the things which thou hast learned and hast been assured of, knowing of whom thou hast learned them; And that from a child thou hast known the holy scriptures, which are able to make thee wise unto salvation through faith which is in Christ Jesus. All scripture is given by inspiration of God, and is profitable for doctrine, for reproof, for correction, for instruction in righteousness".

Testimony #3

I am thankful to God for His saving grace and how He continues to give me insights so that I can be a blessing to others. As a child of God, He continues to reveal himself to me in dreams, visions and revelations and I am a witness of how God can bless you when you obey His voice.

I can also testify about when the Lord spoke to me in the year 2000. He told me to bring the churches together. Initially, this seemed like a very difficult task but thanks to the Almighty for providing some powerful fathers and mothers of Christ who helped me to fight this battle. This took a lot of hard work and through determination we never gave up as we were confident, we were doing the work of the Lord.

After I received this revelation from God about uniting the churches in my immediate communities, I visited my overseer and presiding Bishop, Lee Harold Walsh to share this direction with him. I ensured that the instructions I was given in the revelation were followed and as a result of this the, *Unity Fasting Group of Churches* was born in March of the year 2000, and today I am blessed by the growth of this organization.

This group of churches meet at different times to fast and pray, and I have seen how God would have been exalted by the work of these noble men and women of God. During these Unity Fasting Services I have witnessed individuals being healed, souls revived and the unity amongst the churches strengthened in significant ways. This group has been an inspiration to me as I continue my journey. The Unity Fasting Group of Churches is a force to be reckoned with. I can testify of the impact of this group throughout the parish of Saint Ann and I am blessed that I listened to the voice of God.

Today, I am grateful that the Unity Fasting Group of Churches hosted an appreciation service on my behalf and I am very appreciative. I must say this is an opportunity not only to celebrate, but to recall, review, renew and recommit. I am thankful to my God for being so good to spare my life to be a part of this momentous day.

I recall receiving so many other revelations from God to visit other places to spread the gospel. I was mentored by the patriarchs in the gospel, so I was not afraid to obey the voice of God. Being sent to these places was like victory already won. I no longer must travel on foot, so this was much easier than in the days when I was evangelizing. The people at times accepted the messages and became closer to God through testimonies while others refused to accept. I felt fulfilled because I delivered the message I was given, as that was what I was sent to do. I want to encourage everyone who God has spoken to, "When the Lord says "go", be obedient. He will take care of anything that happens during the journey, and He will take care of you just follow his command.

Like He said in *__Joshua 1: 9 "Have not I commanded thee? Be strong and of a good courage; be not afraid, neither be thou dismayed: for the Lord thy God is with thee whithersoever thou goest."__*

This God remained so faithful in the past and there is no doubt He will remain the same. The evidence I can recall of God showing up on my missions are many, but these are just the few that stand out in my mind.

HUMILITY IN THE WORK OF CHRIST

As children of God, we may preach boldly, and with great passion however we must stay submissive to the words of God, if He is to be pleased with the work we do. We can be firm but remain humble as humility does not mean being, "wishy washy" but being mindful of the other, meek and not being proud. Paul wrote to the brethren at Philippians:

Philippians 2:3-5 Let nothing be done through strife or vain glory; but in lowliness of mind let each esteem other better than themselves. Look not every man on his own things, but every man also on the things of others. Let this mind be in you, which was also in Christ Jesus:

In order for us to focus on this journey and to be a part of the work of Christ, we must learn to be humble. Respect those in authority and in extension God will be pleased with us. If we remain submissive and respectful God will be pleased to have us on his team because He is the head of the church. I say to you men and women who have puffed yourselves and have caused great damage to the Church of God to desist. Look unto Jesus who is by far the greatest example anyone can model, as despite His encounter with death, humbled Himself to the cross.

__Philippians 27:7-8 "But made himself of no reputation, and took upon him the form of a servant, and was made in the likeness of men: And being found in fashion as a man, he humbled himself, and became obedient unto death, even the death of the cross".__

PURPOSE

Like the architect in his task to construct a dwelling has to prepare a plan, so our Father God designs us intentionally with a blueprint, like He mentioned in:

Jeremiah 29:11 "For I know the thoughts that I think toward you, saith the Lord, thoughts of peace, and not of evil, to give you an expected end".

The truth is, like our successes God often designs or allows difficulties in our lives. He does so in order to work out His intentions for us and to strengthen us in our trust and confidence in His power to provide answers. God's plans and intent for every one of us is not by accident; He is deliberate with what He does. Trust God's purpose, and you will be surprised at the end results you realize.

A NOTE TO THE CHURCH

It is with pleasure that I present this message of congratulations and greetings to the churches. I must commend you all for the wonderful work you all continue to do in ensuring that we reach the lost at any cost. There is still much work for us to do to ensure that God's Kingdom is enhanced and that we stand together in unity. God is depending on all of us to stand and be counted.

I encourage the churches to continue to pray together and uphold holiness throughout your assemblies. Do not let down your guards and do not slumber in the spirit, because you all know that the adversary the devil is on the hunt for your souls. We all have a responsibility to stand out in our communities and not be afraid to carry out the work of God as stated in the gospel of

John 9: 4, "I must work the works of him that sent me, while it is day: the night cometh, when no man can work."

Just as God stood with Joshua when he was appointed in Moses stead so the God we serve today will defend you:

(Joshua 1:5-7) **"There shall not be any man be able to stand before thee all the days of thy life as I was with Moses so shall I be with thee. I will not fail thee nor forsake thee. Be strong and be of good courage, for unto this people shall thou divide for an inheritance the land, which I swore unto their fathers to give them, Only be thou strong and very courageous, that thou mayest observe to do according to all the law which Moses my servant commanded thee".**

Our mission will end at different times based on Gods timing for our lives. As individuals in the church It is our duty to continue to work in all steadfastness, to accomplish the reward promised which is eternal life. Let Us continue to work together, ***"endeavoring to keep the unity of the Spirit in the bond of peace."(Ephesians 4:3)***

Today, I am happy I answered the call of God and I thank all my mothers and fathers of the gospel who held my hands and helped me even when I was not doing right. Be that kind friend to someone in the church, and provide the support for them so they can stay on the True Vine. We are workers together for God so we cannot allow the bond to break. I remember where I am coming from I could be called a scoffer at the church window and now I am transformed to a servant of God. Do not dilute the word of God in the name of friendship or fame but stand on the precepts of God and be supportive to all. Hold the hands of the weak, the discouraged, the frail, the strong and teach them how to grow, because that is how the Lord treated us.

I exhort you like Paul did to the brethren : "Set your mind on things above and allow your ministry to be so guided. The ***PEACE OF GOD BE WITH YOU ALL.***

FOCUS ON THE FINISH LINE

This journey is not an easy one, but I have learnt that despite everything I encountered I must keep my eyes on the finish line. I have been fortunate that through the spirit my God has allowed me to view the finish line before my journey ends. I have my eyes being focused on the finishing line and I will not be focused on the distractions and the discouragements that I face as I trod.

The finish line is the fulfilment of my purpose or reward for the special call God has on my life. We can only accomplish these if during our journey we listen to the voice of God, grow in wisdom, understand discernment and remain humble then we will make it to the finishing line. When we are called by God and understand that we are selected for His divine will, we will stay true to Him. Our salary, circumstances or conditions may change but the purpose God has for us will never change. With this acknowledgement we will make it to the finishing line, because our God" promises are sure He never changes, He is still the same yesterday and forever.

My friends, it is important for you to choose daily to get up and pursue the finish line because that is the goal, we hope to accomplish on this journey we call life. We cannot start this journey and give up after a few miles. Giving up should never be an option because it is at the end you will receive the prize. Let nothing prevent you from obtaining the reward that God has secured for you His child: He is counting on you. As you travel endeavor to keep your eyes on God, the Master. Maintain a good heart, activate the right attitude and a godly character because these are important in ensuring you finish the race successfully.

Hebrews 12:2 "Looking unto Jesus the author and finisher; who for the joy that was set before him endured the cross, despising the shame and is set down at the right hand of the throne of God".

I exhort each child of God to, "Set your affection on things above, not on things on the earth. For ye are dead, and your life is hid with Christ in God."

Pastor Jabu Hlongwane, **an acclaimed singer, songwriter and producer** was inspired to compose the song, *"Keep me true Lord Jesus"* The words are encouraging and should be our request of God ….*There's a race that I must run, there's a victory to be won, give me power, every hour…Keep me true, Keep Me True.*

It is very easy to run a race if the other competitors do not have track records of being very quick on their feet, but it is another thing to be up against individuals who you know are much faster than you. In the Kingdom of God however, we need not worry about who is known for running fast or who is known for being slow. ***What is critical on this journey is endurance.***

You may ask yourself the question:
1. Do I have the will to press on even when the storms in my life are tumultuous?
2. Do I have the strength to press on even when I meet on obstacles of different sorts?
3. Can I persist to the end even though sickness takes over my body and I am in pain?

O yes you can. I encourage you. " You can, Don't stop pressing forward, because it is at the end you will reap the everlasting promise".

Matthew 24:13 "But he that shall endure unto the end, the same shall be saved".

Don't you ever forget that even when the journey seems tiresome and impossible you are not alone. When it seems like the problems of life are flooding you, you can Hide in Him and find comfort in the Master of the Seas.

I just thought of a song from way back. I don't know if there are any more verses to it or not but these are songs that I use to lighten my burden and I encourage you to sing along with me".

In that Rock I'll hide.
In His shadow I will abide
When the storms of life come sweeping over me
In that Rock I'll hide…………

Again I encourage anyone reading this book to_: "Sing on, Sing on my sisters and brothers ….
Sing on…. Sing"_

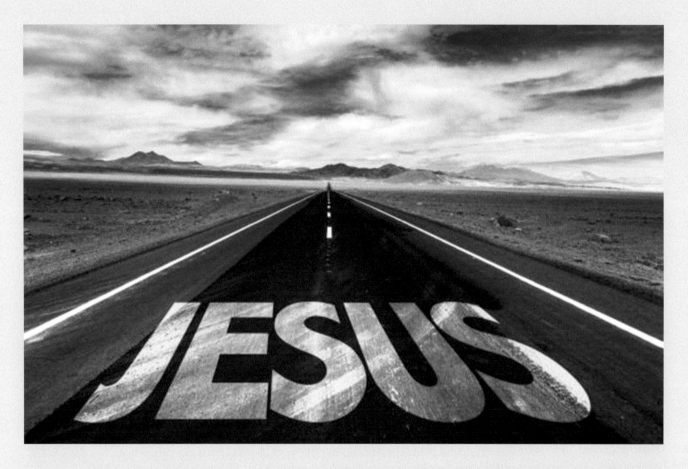

I am fascinated by this journey I am on, knowing that what lies ahead is greater and more profitable than what I am receiving now. I am confident that when I reach that pearly white city that John saw coming down, I shall reap the benefits of being on this journey. This journey that caused me pain, laughter, discouragement, accomplishments, and suffering at times, will be worth it if I endure to the end.

Paul in 2 Corinthians 4:17, presents: "*__For our light affliction, which is but for a moment, worketh for us a far more exceeding and eternal weight of glory__*".

All the experiences I have had help to build my character and heightens my hope in Christ. I am satisfied that God has allowed me this opportunity, so it is up to me to continue with integrity and stay focused.

Like Job I have to water my faith with the love of God so that I can resist the temptations and allow my mind to be peaceful and stayed on God.

Isaiah 26:31 "Thou wilt keep him in perfect peace, whose mind is stayed on thee: because he trusteth in thee".

I encourage everyone to be mindful of this mission you are on and keep your eyes on God who is the ultimate gift.

Your journey may be filled with thistles and seem long and perilous. Like Job, you may encounter many disappointments that will cause you great discomfort, but hold on to your integrity, fertilize your faith with the words of God and complete with patience the journey you are on. The passage to you obtaining life everlasting or damnation may vary; I encourage you to do everything possible to reap the reward that God promises. You must be determined, steadfast, true, and patient and ensure this journey is completed successfully.

Deuteronomy 10::11 "And the LORD said unto me, Arise, take [thy] journey before the people, that they may go in and possess the land, which I swore unto their fathers to give unto them".

God's promises stand sure, so we should rest on the assurance we have in Him. The scripture: Psalm 23:2-3 was revealed to me, and I want to encourage you accordingly,

Psalm 23:2-3 "He maketh me to lie down in green pastures: he leadeth me beside the still waters. He restoreth my soul: he leadeth me in the paths of righteousness for his name's sake".

GETTING TO THE FINISHING......

As I bring the curtains down on me sharing a part of my journey, I am reminded of the song done by the Dewey's entitled, Heavens Sounding Sweeter.

Heavens Sounding Sweeter all the time.
Seems like lately it's always on my mind
Someday I'll leave this world behind, cause heavens sounding sweeter all the time.

Every living being is on a journey. It may not seem so but think about it. When we were born our life started at a particular time and place and throughout time will end at another stage and place. That's a journey... "A travel from one place to another." Life to me is certainly a journey, but how we traverse the route is what is very important. Some individuals decide to just travel without any care or concern about how or where the journey will end, but others like myself are concerned about the entire route including the destination. The decision we make is sometimes based on how we were socialized or there are many instances where through divine experience. Revelation or inspiration we make the sound decision to allow the Saviour, Christ Jesus, on this mission.

Today, I am really happy I invited Christ on this life's mission, because I would not be able to make it thus far. I am happy that as I draw closer to the finish line I can declare like David in:

<u>Psalm 92:12, "The righteous shall flourish like the palm tree: he shall grow like a cedar in Lebanon."</u>

I am on the homestretch, and I am**<u>, "Being confident of this very thing, that he which hath begun a good work in you will perform it until the day of Jesus Christ" (Philippians 1:6)</u>**

That's the promise my travelling companion made with me through His Holy words, and I am positive that He will honour it. The ending of the journey has been difficult, but I am not surprised that the adversary the devil will not let me off the hook. What he does not realize is that like Paul encouraged the church in *1 Corinthians 10:13,* the message is still potent and applicable:

"There hath no temptation taken you but such as is common to man: but God is faithful, who will not suffer you to be tempted above that ye are able; but will with the temptation also make a way to escape, that ye may be able to bear it."

Then my soul shall fear no ill, let Him lead me where He will. I will go without a murmur and His footsteps follow still. (Author: Fanny J. Crosby)

My recommendation however to you all is to ensure that you make the decision to not travel without a friend who will provide the support you need to the end. I did not start this mission with that knowledge of God, but overtime I saw where my life was headed, and I chose to have my friend with me.

The Saviour With Me by Author: Fanny J. Crosby

"I must have my Saviour with me, for I dear not walk alone. I must feel His presence near me and His arms around me throne. Then my soul shall fear no I'll let Him lead me where He will, I will go without a murmur and His footsteps follow still."

Today, I lift my hope in the God who has been my traveling partner. He has been such a true friend to me, and I want to recommend Him to anyone who feels: alone, like your life has not been fulfilling, like you are not doing well, like you are on a journey, hopeless or whatever other emotions you are feeling. **I recommend Jesus to you.**

Do not end this mission all by yourself because you will need the Savior with you. The Lord Jesus is important because through His teachings, peace, and the examples he demonstrated we will be able to face our trials, change our lives and move in confidence with Him. Let me say this: everything in this life has an expiration date, likewise everything has a resumption date. That period between the resumption and the expiration is our journey. One day our journey will end, and we will commence everlasting life with the creator, or everlasting turmoil. The decision is ours. Like Adam and Eve decided to disobey while they were in the garden and sin entered the world, so it is important to ensure the decision we make affect us positively. Think on these things my brothers and sisters, please think on these things.

I am confident in the hope that one day I will see Him and reign with Him, because that is His promise to mankind. The decision I made many years ago will impact my transition, so a*s I near my destination my brothers and sisters I am comforted by the words from*

2nd Timothy 4: 87-8: "Henceforth there is laid up for me a crown of righteousness, which the Lord, the righteous judge, shall give me at that day: and not to me only, but unto all them also that love his appearing."

My brothers and sisters, that is the hope I have in Christ Jesus, and I am anticipating His reward. This is the inheritance, Paul did not just say the reward was for him alone, but as Christians we must be encouraged because this prize is for, ***"all them also that love his appearing."***

I encourage the children of God to keep your eyes focused on God. You may have a long way to go, or you may be on the homestretch, it doesn't matter. Your eyes must be stayed on Christ in order for you to accomplish your heavenly reward. (... ***"Eye hath not seen, nor ear heard, neither have entered into the heart of man the things that God hath prepared for them that love Him...." 1 Corinthians 2:9)***

It makes no sense you spend sleepless nights working for God and at the end you are disappointed. Stay the course and watch out for the ***"Googly Balls"*** my brothers and sisters. These will come directly to throw us off course even as we try to make it to the finish line. Listen now, it is the unexpected obstructions that will deter us, but keep your eyes upon your target and be vigilant. Stay firm in your calling and your faith in Jesus Christ. Listen to His voice instructing you and I am sure like I anticipate; you will be able to declare like ***Paul in*** 2ⁿᵈ **Timothy 4:7-8**

"I have fought a good fight, I have finished my course, I have kept the faith: Henceforth there is laid up for me a crown of righteousness, which the Lord, the righteous judge, shall give me at that day: and not to me only, but unto all them also that love his appearing".

Peace be unto you my brethren, and the love of God be dispersed in your hearts forever. May his goodness provide a route for your steps daily, and His favors circulates your entire being. I pray you all receive a just reward and bask in the inheritance God promises.

In the Name of Jesus, my Lord and Saviour. Amen.......Amen

Gloria Patricia Stephenson pictured here praying at the service of recognition held in her honor by the Unity Fasting Group of Churches at Clyesdale Apostolic Church.

TO GOD BE THE GLORY, GREAT THINGS HE HAS DONE. AMEN, AMEN.

Printed in the United States
by Baker & Taylor Publisher Services